Comparisons

&

Conversions

Also by Harry Guest

Poetry
A Different Darkness
The Achievements of Memory
Mountain Journal
The Hidden Change
A Puzzling Harvest (*Collected Poems 1955–2000*)

Novels
Days
Lost Pictures
Time After Time

Radio Plays
The Inheritance
The Emperor of Outer Space

Translations
Post-War Japanese Poetry (with Lynn Guest and Kajima Shôzô)
The Distance, The Shadows (66 Poems by Victor Hugo)
Versions
From a Condemned Cell (33 Sonnets by Jean Cassou)

Non-Fiction
Another Island Country
Mastering Japanese
Traveller's Literary Companion to Japan
The Artist on the Artist

HARRY GUEST

Comparisons

&

Conversions

Shearsman Books
Exeter

First published in the United Kingdom in 2009 by
Shearsman Books Ltd
58 Velwell Road
Exeter EX4 4LD

ISBN 978-1-84861-019-4

Acknowledgements
'At the Tomb of Chateaubriand' was first printed in *Lost and Found*
(Anvil Press Poetry, London, 1983) and subsequently in
A Puzzling Harvest (Anvil, 2002). Thanks to Anvil Press Poetry for
permission to reproduce the poem here.
'The Death of Pindar' was included in *The Artist on the Artist*
(Elm Bank Publications, Exeter, 2000).
Grateful acknowledgement is due to *Agenda* and *The Journal* in which
other texts in *Conversions* first appeared.

Contents

COMPARISONS

A Travel Log

for Lynn, ideal companion

Early evening. Spread over its hi-jacked crater
the city's glitter's muted under dregs of smog.
Eighteen thousand feet. Our starboard wing
glides past the tapering summit of a brown
volcano—not shining as in Turner's poem
since fresh lava's smeared the snow off. Two
miles of air to fall through till we face
the future on solid ground. In the event
terra proves somewhat less than firma during
the optimistic trek to claim our luggage
for a minor tremor makes the airport windows
rattle. Then frantic traffic. Church doors gape
to show quivering candles. In this muggy
November shirtsleeved men on the sidewalk
fry tortillas. At sunrise from the fifteenth floor
we peer down on a flat roof piled with fir-cones.

At Guadalupe the Old Basilica's lopsided.
This crater used to be a lake. Buildings here
tend to tilt and sink. We tiptoe warily under
iffy-looking arches clamped with metal struts
remembering that church in Venice whose
crypt is permanently floored with water,
the altar standing on itself reversed in murk.
Quite near St. Mark's. Tasha, intrepid, ran along
those scary galleries inspecting the mosaics.
I followed cautiously whereas you and Nick
stayed earthbound on marble.
                              The New
Basilica's thronged splendidly for Mass.
An unstressed subtext of the Vision surely means
that in the pauper Mary had already found
the most important person in the land. No need
to winkle out a viceroy or a bishop as
that peasant filled the bill. And whether one believes

9

in the miraculous roses is of secondary
importance—like tossing evidence about
the Turin Shroud from scientific hand to hand
since intellect and epiphanies belong so far
apart that any truths get fumbled in
between.

         The Mayans thought gold was the sweat
of the sun and silver the tears of the moon.
Japanese eyes detect a hare in the lunar disc
and Ray Bradbury's rocket-ship sought to scoop
out incandescent gobs of solar matter
conveying a few of Yeats's golden
apples back to earth. The haphazard
quality of my early education meant
I never had to study chemistry
or physics yet at Teotihuacán
the Pyramid of the Moon mimics the contour
of a mountain to the north. I looked down
from halfway up the steps to an enigmatic
quadrangle with low partitions in each corner
open towards the centre. A photograph
caught you exploring the south-east wall not
glancing up when I waved. From that plaza
it's half a mile and down a slope to reach
the Pyramid of the Sun but the designers
made sure both platforms stand at precisely
the same height. Two Swallowtails flicked by
brilliant on the hot wind. You didn't ascend
this structure either. Hard-going, actually.
Grabbing hold of the steep rope as youths red-
shirted for a Sunday outing leapt past
jeering at shrieks of terror from their girls.
The sky extended cloudless but alas clogged
molecules of fumes concealed the two volcanic
landmarks. From Tokyo in the sixties

Fuji too loomed visible for just a few days
each New Year when the factories had closed—
then, gradually, through January, its white cone
went back to non-existence beyond haze.
Last August though each evening we could see
its dark triangle block some stars from the roof-bar
of that improbable hotel in Shinagawa
with five thousand rooms. On our second stay,
after that conference on the coast where I'd
run seminars about Ole Ez, I went
down to the shop for whisky, postcards
and o-sembei. Then could not recall the number
of our new room nor which one of the three
skyscrapers we were lodged in. "Sumimasen.
Heya no bangô wa wasurechatta ga."
The lass at Reception was sympathetic.
Accepted I was speaking Japanese
without releasing even a single giggle
one slim hand fanned up to protect her mouth.

Off in the bus to visit Shôzô, dear
poet-scholar-painter in his lush highland
fastness. At noon we passed the flank of Fuji
as cinnamon as Hokusai showed it menaced
by a most unlikely lightning-flash. In Shô's
wild garden irises and a persimmon-tree,
the skyline circled by dark green mountains.
Each day we walked to a spring with nonstop water
delectable as that torrent in the Mani
crashing into a stone trough under Taygetos
to slake wayfarers for at least three thousand
years. We were driving back from the majestic
remains of Mystras scattered on the slope
beneath the fort. A fresco in the Pantanassa
shows two Kings only heading for the stable—

one on a blue horse, one on a red, several
centuries before Franz Marc. Off on a fruitful
tangent one would hope. A bunch of grapes
dangling from a spar in some surrealist
geometry.
          But back to Mexico
a year ago, accompanied again by you,
the shadowy other, my private vocative,
that second person singular of wedlock.
A light plane started slanting round to land
showing that longed-for flattened hill set so
symmetrically with ruins. Oaxaca
itself guards memories of Lowry—Malcolm
not L.S. although it could be intriguing
to place Lancastrian matchstick-figures clad
in broadcloth on sunstruck plazas. My Penguin
copy of *Dark As The Grave* contains a misprint:
Parker's *place* for *Piece*. Understandable
for readers unacquainted with that patch
of green in Cambridge. In Lowry's novel
SIGBJØRN and PRIMROSE (no kidding) get lost
attempting to walk up to Monte Albán.
We were more fortunate. Its graceful plan's
rectangular, north-south, with one perhaps
observatory at odds with other structures—
a blunt-built arrowhead directed at
a special colony of the nighttime sky.
As elegant a site as Copán flown to
by a "crate" Biggles would have been proud
to take up. On the runway, chocks really did
get whipped away. In that Honduran canyon
the flaking wings seemed likely any second
to scrape against the cliffs on either side.
The terminal by the tufted landing-field
boasted a thatched roof. We hung around

and spied bright birds with no names. A yellow bus
passed shady gardens where naked children
smiled and waved, forded a stream as jolly
families were laving their jalopies,
squealed at last to a halt: Ruinas
de Copán. A dusty square. Gaunt donkeys
tethered. Men, dark eyes hidden under wide-
brimmed hats, clenched thin cigars between gold teeth.
Two tame macaws summed us up from a fence
when we bought tickets but we'd seen as vivid ones
flying over that river at dusk, the snout
of a crocodile breaking the surface as if
to contradict my prep school master who
contended cacti and alligators belong
to The New World, crocs and succulents being
prerogative of The Old. Arid pastures
to the south did let cactus-hedges protect
ochre soil. Black vultures floated like scraps
of burnt paper. In *The Power and the Glory*
Greene compares them to indigestion-spots.
Going over the Sierra Madre we must have
crossed the route taken by the whisky-priest
(not named) dogged by the lieutenant
(equally lacking a label) who stood
for the steelgrey power of the secular state
unable nonetheless to stifle the glory
of the oh so unworthy martyr but who am I
to measure worthiness? How can I gauge
the virtues or demerits of an action
undergone by others? It's hard enough
to end each day recalling where I've failed,
how often and so unforgivably. That's why
we journey on, hoping by space to leave
the faults of time behind but men seem bound
to loop back like a boomerang lobbed deftly

to similar commissions of despair.
Gloom-thoughts to be going on with. Let's
click back consolingly to visiting
that church in Zinancantán. Broken free
from the establishment it's run by shamans.
We sidled in, welcomed indifferently.
Men were busy carpeting the entire
floor with dry pine-needles. Luckily no-one
jogged any of the many flickering candles.
One part-time deacon reverently traced the outline
of a kneeling supplicant with two eggs held
by thumb and middle-finger symbolising
rebirth into crowing health. He then dosed
his patient with Coca-Cola. The gas helps
to expel evil spirits. (On a wall
in Cartersville, Georgia, they've preserved
a huge advertisement for this beverage
painted in the 1890s. Its usefulness
for exorcism doesn't rate a mention.)
Despite their apostasy, they've retained
effigies of accepted saints—the one
nearest the high altar is the main target
for their prayers. If there's no response,
he's banished to the west end of the queue.
After a sound thrashing.

                Our Tokyo landlord
used ceremoniously to berate the parental
ashes kept in bronze urns on a scarlet tansu.
That room was shadowed by his pride and joy—
a banana-tree shrouded in winter
with coconut sacking. Its jagged leaves
drooped exactly as Bashô described them—
like the injured tail of a phoenix. (Neither
he nor I can vouch for the accuracy
of the comparison.) It's been cut down.

So has the orange-tree whose foliage,
aglow with uneatable fruit in December,
darkened the room in which the children played
listening to EPs of Moomin or (Nichol's
favourite) *The Grand Canyon Suite* by Grofé.
One strict rule. Toys at bathtime put away
behind the uncomfortable sofa so parents
(each doubtless clutching a replenished glass)
could cross the yellow carpet in stockinged feet
without tripping over a kettledrum, Noah's
Ark, Ultraman in two sizes, chipped lorries,
grey scabbard (long swordless), a white furry
bear daubed for some reason with green paint,
block letters of the alphabet, a top
which used to whine a song, slippery cards
displaying ethnic costumes or painful
pieces of Lego. The other Tzotzil church
placed horses and jaguars of wood at random
near the entrance to the chancel. We trod
just as carefully.
                    Back in the colonial
hotel—Spanish-style patio, the cool trickle
of a fountain—I wondered at the ironclad
conquerors, what they replaced, the whole
repeated shift of violence again
replacing violence. Everywhere we go
we're told of suffering victims and were *they*
worthy or unworthy? No focus merely on
what looks symmetrical when hearts got prised
still throbbing from the rib-cage. Even rulers
pierced their own tongues and penises to make
a gift of agony to the rain-withholding gods
who thrived on blood. I'm squeamish, try
to censor off the cruelty. Truth though (some
of the time) will out. Like honesty. As Lewis

(C.S. not Wyndham) pointed out, each now-gleaming
temple in the Ancient World formed a sacred
abattoir and reeked of blood. At least
the heifer Keats saw on that Grecian urn
stays safe from harm. Indifferent centuries
have cleansed those altars and obliterated
screams as feathered priests hurled captives, wrists
and ankles lashed, down the cliff-flight of steps
like ones at Tikal jutting from the jungle
canopy where howler monkeys loll. A dead
fer-de-lance lay by the shadowed wayside
and our guide peered round unhappily in case
its mate should still be lurking.
                              At Paestum
the meadows look as if they had been groomed
in preparation for Persephone's bare
feet to walk there hardly dinting the golden
asphodels but sacrificial slabs
give off the unsniffed stench of animals
selected for their beauty for the knife.
A modern hypocrite, I'm able guiltily
to choose the ambience I seek to see
and don't allow the proof humanity
gawps happily at different ways to maim
or kill both beasts and its own kind to spoil
my pleasure at the architecture, mar
craving for a safe dream. Once, to my shame,
I saw kick-boxing in Bangkok. Back in Japan
on the grey-blue TV screen, it had seemed
like a rather sexy ballet. The real thing
was different. I left, sickened by
yells of protest when a bout was stopped.
One of the contestants had been badly hurt
and the spectators wanted him to go on
getting hurt.

How can a supposedly
civilised nation like France venerate
their squalid revolution? Day in day out
the mob would jeer when people like themselves
(or better) got guillotined. Howled with delight
when dripping heads held by the hair were asked
to give their name. Women sat knitting close
by the carnage to smell the fear, savour
those endless acts of barbarism, tot up
each splash of human blood.
                                   Why can a creed
however primitive believe the gods
who made men wanted men to kill their fellows?
How to build a useful bridge over the marsh.
First find your victim. Stun him. Drown him. Bang
in the initial pile. That prehistoric
Irishman with well-kept fingers was maimed
abominably when still alive then left
to suffocate in mud. He reached a hand
across millennia, in anguish, out to
the archaeologist who couldn't tell
why either.
                 The urge to know. Look behind
a motive, scrutinise the dice or track
the direction taken by a crow. Check
Palenque steamy after downpour. The tower
(unmatched elsewhere) could never have been seen
by the plebs out there on the scraped plaza.
So the presumed elect at work deciphering
counsels of cloud or moon pondered unwatched,
aloof, unmonitored. Who'd challenge, verify
what had been glimpsed or when? At Stonehenge
or Carnac one assumes night's prodigies
got studied in the open, communally—smear
of brilliance (Hale-Bopp before its time)

or just a star which suddenly wasn't
there. Arcane discoveries tend to be hoarded
by the few. Then there's that itch to keep somehow
in contact with the dead. In 1952
Lhuillier took months removing
rubble from a stairway leading down
to the funerary chamber. A long narrow
tube of stone brought air although the monarch's
nose lay beneath a mask of green jade squares.
The hole in Trethevy Quoit is wider
though showing the same wish for an airy
link to the lair of the corpse to allow
a whiff of consoling pollen, memory
of outside rain or (on Bodmin) the scentless
sense of frost—or, once again, perhaps
a nagging hope for a two-way natter
with the familiar departed? At one end
rotting lips in darkness and at the other
an ear warmed by sunlight clamped to the stone
receiver.
      Alone up the first flight of steps
on any structure awe increases till I reach
a ledge, veers giddily to wonder when
I probe moist shadows in the temple proper—
not so much probably to comprehend
as celebrate the literally higher
mysteries. At Tikal having scrambled up
one derelict pyramid in the 'Lost World' complex
I stood by the doorless box of stone
and nearly tumbled back down the crumbling steps
for a vulture flapped screeching past my shoulder
with the black effect of a long-disused
umbrella shaking off a residue of mould.
Angkor, before the foulness of Pol Pot,
proved vultureless but just as sheer in the dry

time before the monsoon spewed relief and so
the lake at Neak Pean spread as withered grass
(though slender boys stripped to the waist sluiced
cattle in the river near Siem Reap). There's
fascination in a island you can walk to—
the sandstone lotus should appear to be
floating on water but my photograph
shows it abandoned, fading on the film,
while a white-hatted Japanese family
is filing towards it treading on mauve turf.
Tasha, aged three, took all her clothes off
in the bar that evening. Nobody appeared
to mind or even notice. Dark lizards
squatted vertically in our room near
the air-conditioner which didn't work.
Under a bronze pre-monsoon sun we went
by pedicab to Angkor Thom and paced
the Terrace of the Leper King, setting
for Debussy's moonlit audiences. To skulk
at nighttime there and watch with such unease
the pallor make the carvings seem to stir.
There would be snakes though slithering
chromatically across the cooling flagstones.
At Edzná lately I prowled by myself
climbing to a platform where a ruined wall
formed a kind of crenellation. Despite
December heat in Yucatán I froze.
A blunt yellow head peered through one space. Eight
feet to the left a tail protruded. It liked
the look of me even less than I of it and slid
away. In Connecticut as a child I knew
blacksnakes thrived in my aunt's silver-birchwood.
Copperheads too. And rattlers. None,
I'm glad to say, at Angkor. Coming from
Hong Kong we'd flown over a war. You saw

smoke-puffs here and there among the dense-set trees
where U.S. and Korean troops were attempting
to eliminate the Viet Cong. And vice versa.
The stewardess plucked Nichol, then eight months,
from my lap and strode off to show him
to the Japanese pilot. Crossing our fingers
we envisaged glad hands leaving the joystick
to grab a blond gaijin-baby ("kawaii")
while the plane unguided took a nosedive
to the disputed land. Outside the Palace
in Phnom Penh (close to the stables for the royal
elephants) they'd placed an American plane
brought down their side of the frontier despite
Nixon's repeated claim there were no flights
over Cambodia.

           As Costa Rica has
no armed forces now, they've commandeered
the barracks in San José to form a fine
museum. Some fantastic small altars
found in deepest jungle prove how anywhere
will serve as a place for worship and to lay
offerings for whatever gods may swirl
unseen between lianas and mossed trunks
to take a peek at mortal life but give no hint
of what might happen after death. Near sea-
level there whereas that sacred area in
Peru at fifteen thousand feet still gets
clambered up to by devout Indians. No
vegetation. Dark rock all round. Snow patches.
Our lungs sucked shallow air as we tramped
uncomprehendingly with reverence
to the high precinct walled off by boulders.
Still loftier peaks white-glistening formed a ring
of distance—two allowing pale smoke to drift
across a faultless sky, unyielding, blue,

hard-seeming as enamel. One August,
fleeing the Kantô summer, Dennis and I,
abandoning our wives and offspring, climbed
Mount Asama. Foolhardy, ill-equipped,
ripping our gym-shoes (can you imagine)
on pumice. Stood brushed by sullen fumes
gazing down into the slumbering crater
which reeked of rotten eggs. At Arenal
red-hot rocks came bouncing down from the summit
swathed in cloud leaving a grubby wake
of steam that hissed to nothingness. Spanish
orchids, vermilion, golden, grew sporadic
on the roughened wasteland. A subdued
continual roar. A dizzy sense the ground
was paper-thin. And sprawling Poas
attained via a forest stuck with epiphytes
and eco-poems rather vapidly nailed
to the occasional branch. You suggested,
smiling sweetly, I should add one but I,
ignoring irony, felt eager to reach
the ledge and peer down at the glaucous lake
an evil mist uncoiling from its surface.
Our landlord's son drove us halfway up Fuji.
I found a chunk of igneous rock the size
of a cricket-ball lying now beside
a pinkish lump to prove I'd either been
on top of Asama or low down on
the slopes of Mauna Loa near that grey tunnel
fern-hung where coursing lava had slowly cooled
not all that long ago. I would like to know
for certain which is which. Remembrance
blurs. I'm no geologist.
                              Sea-level once
again. The Inland One. Littered with islands
between Shikoku and Honshû. I first

saw Miyajima in Paris as a student
waiting to catch the last train home for Easter.
The film *The Gate of Hell*. That torii
majestic on posters in the Métro
lured one to risk a crimson gate to nowhere
set up in the sea. Though it was fifteen years
before I saw it in three dimensions—shortly
after Nick, aged four, had been sent flying
by a deer disgruntled for no apparent reason
in the shrine park. *Tori-i*. For birds to perch
on or, more accurately, be. The faithful
hurl pebbles up to see if prayers are answered.
Should one land on the crossbar it's good luck.
At low tide a scattering of stones reveals
how tricky it is to make the gods respond.
There've been good secular pilgrimages, the first
as a schoolboy on a borrowed bike
past scrawny vineyards in Touraine to see
the manor where Ronsard lived, imagine him,
so deaf, plucking down for emblems seven stars
to re-invent French poetry in sounds
of such inventive symmetry. To Bemerton
where Herbert preached and meditated,
prayed and wrote. From the village you see the spire
of Salisbury across what used to be
water-meadows. Frost and his wife lie east
of that tall white church in New England.
The inscription on the tombstone reads
"Together wing to wing and oar to oar".
A nice museum close by shows some sly
primitives by Grandma Moses. Norman
Rockwell lived for a time near a covered bridge
also in Vermont and painted as a girl a
charming old lady in the gallery there who'd
hardly changed at all. Two years ago,

amazed to find clean water rolling down
the Sumidagawa treasured by Kafû,
we didn't struggle through wet heat of August
to visit his Peony Garden but could walk
along the new cemented river-path
to pay respects to a statue of Bashô.
Last spring, helped by friendly strikers
from the nuclear power-station at La Hague
(they held French cars up but, cheering, waved us on)
we found the churchyard where Prévert is buried.
In '93 Josyph, Rudolf and I—
fellow Hawthornden Fellows in a chilled
November—did homage on a rare day of clear sky
to William Drummond whose hospitality
we were enjoying at his castle—not
imitating Ben Jonson who came on foot
all the way from London but trudging over
snow from my parked car. The tomb itself's
a strange unwindowed chapel with a roof
of weighty rectangular slabs.
                              It can't be
ghoulish, surely, to seek out graves of those
whom one admires. Pianists leave fragrant wreaths
for Chopin before giving a recital
and validate that difficult two-way phrase
"communion of saints" from the Apostles'
Creed at Evensong. It's hard to grasp
why time and again faceless asses desecrate
the somewhat tasteless tomb of Oscar Wilde also
in Père Lachaise—by no means as impressive
as Maggie Hambling's stone settee. Fanatic
"homophobes" presumably. Unlike Wilde
(who begged the Oxford examiners to let
him go on with his translation of the Gospel
because he wanted to see how it would end)

I'm no Greek scholar but that queer coinage
must only mean "fear of the same". So are
those vandals afraid they'd glimpse themselves
tangled in a tell-tale mirror? Rather
a give-away. And so there is a quirky
virtue in pedantry.
                            At the Eraion
one hot day we forked out several drachmai
(I phoned for the plural to a classicist)
to a student needing a shave who sat
hunched in a sort of sentry-box absorbed
by his tattered comic before wandering
past the ribbed stumps of columns. An arid wind
blew over Argos, over the thorned and scented plain
where Homer asserted that the horses grazed.
The site lies on three levels, topmost just
a barren floor. The temple got burned down
by a drowsy priestess. And not much more
to see high on Paros. Stones among pine-trees
mark Poseidon's temple where the taxi waited,
thin chickens strut and where Demosthenes
took poison with a view of the near sea.
By bus to a serene monastery, the precinct
flamed by dark immobile cypresses.
A British ensign in the retinue
of some ambassador died here of fever.
The words on his grave are carved with a touching
inaccuracy as the stonemason had been
unfamiliar with the Roman alphabet.
In the early sixties two colleagues and I
took a posse of boys to Greece. Descending
the gangplank at Dunkirk they noticed
a restaurant where the apple-pies
"are just like momma make" but we had
a train to catch. Through Yugoslavia

brown peatsmoke purling past the windows blurred
minarets and swarthy characters waiting
in curly-toed slippers by each level-
crossing. The barman accepted half-crowns. Just
one procured three fierce glasses of slivovitz.
For members of staff. When we weren't in the bar
the boys doubtless negotiated the same
deal. After two days of travel Athens station.
A terminus blocking a single line. Grass
grew between the rails. The platform I recall
was made of wood. Roger spoke Modern Greek
and coped amazingly. Hotels then cost
the equivalent of five bob a room. Four beds.
He charged the boys (or rather their parents)
thirty-nine quid for the entire fortnight spent
abroad. Victoria to Victoria. Ah.
I too have crossed Arcadia. Strolled
beneath green shadows in Olympia. Watched
eagles wheel above the enigmatic
Tholos at Delphi. Tiryns boasts a bath
apparently resembling the one
Agamemnon took his last dip in. We walked
that April to each site from local buses,
had Mycenae all day to ourselves,
stroked sunwarmed marble, sent hushed echoes round
the beehive tombs in all the luxury
of solitude. Three decades later coaches
were lined up forty deep on shimmering tarmac
outside the Lion Gate. The importunity
of a Japanese guide about to instruct
her gaggle pushed you out of the way
so you almost tumbled over the balustrade
into a deep pit. You had the ability
to reprimand the offender in brisk,
well-chosen Japanese. It stayed unheard

under the blare of the megaphone so we found
in dudgeon the rock-cut corridor along which
Orestes fled down to the wild valley
after matricide.

Returning in '61
we all slept on deck, sailing from Patras
to Bari via Ithaca, fourth class, smuts
falling from the funnel. Old women dressed
in black brought goats on board, tethered them
to the brass rail and milked them noisily
into pails. At night, lights glittering
from Greece stopped. Along the Albanian coast
lay darkness. Hoxha in command. Corfu looked
so appealing. I've heard foul discos now
shriek out cacophony all day long as louts
keep vomiting in the streets. Sick transit. Where's
the gloria mundi gone? The Communists
have thrown out full employment with the bath-
water and embraced our so-called "Western
culture" of commercialism, drug-abuse,
licensed irreverence, a growing gap
between the undeserving rich and those
who can't find work. Things slide from worse to worst
and one's lampooned for saying so. Et cetera.
Et cetera. Yes, I know. Since time began
there's always been a Golden Age forever
in the past and irrecapturable,
most certainly exaggerated or else
slyly concocted after the event.
Lust, too. The way we look back yearningly
at younger selves entwined. How sadly often
the ageing recollection can omit
reluctances or disappointments so as
to heighten the effect of lamplight on
bare skin, dab extra honey on a first

filched kiss or hear a husky voice repeat
words which were never uttered. De la Mare
dubbed memory a "fond deceiver". Yet,
for all the happy slanders, misconceptions
left in the cutting-room, how good at times
to summon up that devious faculty
and black the here and now out while we daydream.

For decades I shunned Iberia. Still, Franco's
atrocities have left their smear. Pass in Granada
the restaurant Lorca frequented and think
how he was murdered. Also the bullrings
disgracing every town. I can't forgive
Cocteau or Picasso for relishing
cruelty committed in the afternoon.
That superficial twit K. Tynan claimed
that "one" (meaning himself) felt no more when
the spear pierces the bull than if a ski
prodded a bank of snow. If there's a Hell,
whenever a Bosch demon, half-pig,
half-wasp, with a head like a kettle, goads him
with a redhot prong he may have come to feel
there is a difference.
                          I came across
a crow, its wing clamped in a rusty trap,
on a field above Nevern. And killed it
with a handy rock hoping this was an act
of mercy, still sick with guilt remembering
the wild look in its eyes.
                          Since reading
Eça de Queiros (*The Maias* every bit as good
as Flaubert's pseudo-sentimental view
of education with just as brilliantly
conceived an end) we've seen the swan-ceiling
at Cintra and that enchanting faery castle

actually *in* the Tagus. An ancient tram
took us to Belém. That cool cloister
with interlacing shadows caressing
the memorial to Pessoa—but one
is not enough. Shouldn't each heteronym
possess his own? A small triumphal arch
for Reis? A ship with stone sails for Campos?
A pastoral frieze for Caeiro—maybe
a shepherd fingering a flute?

                                One cause
for regret in Evora: no time to see
that astonishing cromlech to the west.
I pleaded but I had to be content
with two tantalising postcards, noticing
directions to the place by the roadside
as our minibus headed back to Lisbon
over the sunparched plateau with cranes
roosting on rare distant trees.

                                Tash and I
had better luck on Orkney, able to see,
one rainfree June without a nightfall,
all the chambered tombs on Rousay—Blackhammer,
Taversoe Tuick, Knowe of Yarso . . .
Wonderful names! We picnicked on the cliff
facing Eynhallow hearing seals lined up
on a reef keen / sing / moan / whatever. Then
Unstan, Cuween, Wideford on Mainland.
Maes Howe that fixes the midwinter sun
across that standing stone. The remains
of one neolithic house, a square hearth
in the narrow entry they think was there
for purification. From what, I wonder.
The mind flinches away.

                              Five years before,
alone, I'd sailed to Papa Westray, skirted

the pounding sea to the oldest house in Europe.
To reach the Tomb of the Eagles then
(the farmer discovered claws in abundance—
a clan-token like the dog-cult at Cuween)
I knocked at the farmhouse-door. Now,
there's a spanking new Visitors Centre
before you walk along the cliff-edge counting seals.
At the site an Orkney vole scuttled
away into the vetch. Later, Mine Howe
where the subterranean chambers had been
recently unearthed. Literally. Once
an exciting mention in *The Times*, to-day
you descend in three rapt dimensions via
two stairways past two low curving "rooms"
off to the side. Perhaps a trial passage
to the underworld. Steps for the "well"
at Broch of Howe are unworn. If the motive
was fetching water on a daily basis
they'd have been ground down to a central groove.
Shall I ever get to visit that temple
on the Guatemalan border? You'd go
by boat then thread the cliff-cut labyrinth
mimicking the journey to the netherworld,
the *Inframundo*. There's a decapitated
statue of the Jaguar King. Find the head
somewhere. Replace it. And the world will end.
Shall I see more than its description in
the Michelin? All too soon now I suspect
that sort of wistful voyaging will be
the only option. Depend on narratives
and other people's photographs. No longer
to stand where it's remote and test the past
at first hand. Travel by proxy in a fireside
armchair. Worse, a permanent bed. Or rather
an all too temporary one.

                              Some scenes remain
so vivid in the skull. True epiphanies.
Yet trivia too—the raw materials
of experience. Some you'd love to dredge
up fade before the words to fit them rise
glinting in the bucket. Or else bob up
to hover maddeningly beside paths
of a sleepless night. Forced to study
the inside of your eyelids through scarlet
whorls and sudden flarings, lacking the will
to fight your way to reverie or hope.
Trying to think of nothing, you recall
a phone number. VIGilant 1088.
We moved from there in 1947. Details
you are required by law to memorise
stay unmourned behind a mist. Gardens
in autumn twilight though. Littered leaves.
One bush daubed with silver. Drenched blooms,
drooping, over, skeined with cobwebs. Ghosts
forming from breath condensed. Ice-splinters
poised on the brink. But where? What sun
was that detected simply as a more
luminous smudge among the haze? Note in
adjacent graveyards as you walk how swiftly
you skim through every granite page of death.
Sacred to the memory of ——. The whose
eradicated. No flowers placed on All Souls' Day
for a hundred years. Josiah, beloved
grandfather. His great-grandson is also dead.
Much missed. One marble sickle and a sheaf
sliced in two. Gone to a better place. Long
home. Ceramic blossoms. Smeared angel flaunting
a cracked left wing. Stone torch reversed
still smouldering after six decades. Green gravel
sparkles in each cared-for rectangle.

                                                  As well
to tread more softly round some memories
in case they stir and bare a claw. Grey dust
accumulates on lacquer boxes, finch
of glass, fossils Father found near Tenby,
last year's palm cross, a metal diplodocus
treasured since I was seven. On frames,
steel, wood or gilt, reining pictures in—
Landscape Near Zennor, (half-abstracted, bluegreen,
gorse hinted at, one whisk of light which might
be showing a far gleam of sea), self at 70,
advertisement for a Kabuki play,
time-darkened ancestor on my mother's side—
gold buttons, white jabot, a paymaster
in Nelson's navy who may coincidentally
have served on the same ship as John Guest,
my forebear press-ganged at 17 to fight
on the *Orion* at Trafalgar. Also a red
chunk of petrified wood from a shop *outside*
the Arizona National Park. No single flake
can be purloined from the sacrosanct area.
Tasha, excavating that Iron Age site
by the Euphrates, had to dig each day
under the eyes of Turkish guards, rifles
at the ready.
                      Years back, coming from Florence
in a battered Austin Ten, a colleague
drove us up into the lavender hills
behind Grasse to call on an aged friend
who'd worked with Evans at Knossos before
the First World War. The Greeks, quite rightly,
didn't allow any of the discoveries
to leave Crete unchecked. This fellow (then
an undergraduate) was told to stick
a bronze sword down his trouser-leg. It had,

it was thought, been wielded more or less
successfully by King Minos. All went
as planned. He strolled (stiffly, I imagine)
past the cops and customs-men but, half-
way along the gangplank, stumbled. You can see
the bent blade now in the Fitzwilliam.
Why should the Elgin Marbles though be sent
to Athens? If all museums trundled works back
to their place of origin there'd be no point
in amassing a collection at all. Joyce
coined "Museyroom" and it implies just that:
a space where one can ponder what's been done
by fellow-humans since the start of time
worldwide. Ritual masks. The first inscriptions
in Chinese. Penny-farthings. Persian armour. Still
life, diamond window distorted in a rummer
half full of wine. Neolithic pebbles
fist-sized with eyes rayed as if a child stuck
two suns over a wonky river for
a smile. Rajah's scabbard gem-encrusted
like the lean line of a hull overtaken
by glittering barnacles. I can't get used
to rubies being blue. Green garnets, dark
red sapphires throw presuppositions
awry. To be a would-be pop-group or
a poet wet behind the ears just jam
together two far-fetched unlikelihoods.
Call your slim volume or your rowdy band
Cardboard Moonlight or Blue Marigold.
Oxymoron with the emphasis on moron. That's
unfair! And yet that furry cup-and-saucer,
that flatiron fanged with nails. They've said it all.
Or did. Theseus reacting to the blurb
for *Pyramus and Thisby*: "That is hot ice
and wondrous strange snow."

                                        A first-century
sarcophagus in marble, a door
on its side carved scrupulously ajar.
A meteorite had fallen on Alaska.
They shipped it to New York but the compass
on board wouldn't work. Whatever it was
that metal boulder brought from outer space
proved far too strong. Artefacts from Africa
have copied European imports, summing up
to our embarrassment what seemed to be
"The West" in essence. Coffin. Padlock. Gun.
As if our contribution meant just death,
incarceration and the baleful need
to keep what we possess against all odds.
Wondering natives moulded too a tiny
rocking-chair, domestic, intimate,
waiting to harbour a mother and her child
or father resting after toil—which should
console us once we've wrung collective
hands in guilt for, dash it all, there were so
many positive aspects to "The Empire"—great
sacrifice on the part of all who held
unshaken faith in justice and hygiene.
Forgotten now on slabs gummed to church walls,
dead in their twenties of the midday sun,
blackwater fever or gangrene. History
is many thousand shades of right and wrong.
I pen that confidently having failed
the subject in School Cert, dreaming, during
Geography, of the emerald Nile,
its banks lush with papyrus, threading
long saffron wastes of sand. In '38
an aunt brought me a fez from Cairo which
I wore to bore the family with magic—
a shifty Sidney Greenstreet, Tommy Cooper

before his time—not venturing to hope
I would one day float fezless past palm-trees,
watch cows in the swift twilight swimming back
from their grazing islands to the shore. Big
kingfishers whizzed like those depicted on tomb
walls glimpsed through the wrong end of Lawrence's
telescope. Beyond the fertility-strip
the desert not lone and level for Ozymandias
but duned, uneven, rumpled, interrupted
by surprising outcrops pyramid-shaped.
Perhaps how the idea was culled. At five
a.m. teeth chattering I felt beneath
my feet the ice-cold sand which, once day broke,
would scorch and shimmer as that camel-train came
padding north. The fact you cannot see the joins
at Abu Simbel does not prevent a twinge
of sadness for you're not there thunderstruck
before the real thing. Avebury's as heavy
but hasn't had to move—if ransacked now
and then and built on. As smug inheritors
what will our age deserve in reverence
from those to come?
                          In '41, before Pearl Harbor,
another aunt (I have been blessed with more
than Bertie Wooster) set sail from Rio
bringing me a set of vivid butterflies
flattened behind glass. I've been to Luxor now
pacing that copse of titan-columns where
forty people vanish and you're quite alone—
less delicate maybe than Cordoba hiding
a whole cathedral dwarfed within its maze—
but not yet to Brazil save in one winter
cinema at Margate accompanying
Bette Davis in *Now, Voyager*. Vicarious
journey with a post-war whiff of popcorn.

At Kabah though I saw, alive and fluttering,
an iridescent butterfly with a six-
inch wing-span— just like the one now pressed
to faded cottonwool— and sensed a stab
of joyous recognition stained
with fourth-hand blame: net-wielder / salesman /
purchaser / recipient. Such radiance
ought to be kept free from harm but Gilbert White
and Audubon blithely massacred birds
they intended to examine. The past's
shot through with shimmerings of misery
and praise, remorse, easy excuses, just
as easy castigation, judgements forged
too often with less than half the facts in hand.

In '01, mid-November, the plane had just
shrugged off the coast of Ireland. The captain's
voice. "There's been an incident." Silence spread
quickly as the Boeing turned around. Fuel
colourless as vodka gushed for fully
eight minutes from the wings. Down to poison
the innocent Atlantic so that we
could land in safety at Heathrow. We reached
Manhattan in the small hours where we heard
an aircraft carrying passengers home
to the Dominican Republic had crashed
in Queens. This time no terrorism. No
motive evilly trumped up for random slaughter
by fanatics safely far from the event.
Black question-marks seep nonetheless through
photographs of destruction in next morning's
paper beside the vapid answers phoned in
by reporters. And we assent before
we even turn the page. Condemned by default.
Each reference shuffled cunningly
by time and occasions, rarely by regret.

The going-back's so often a mistake.
Though not to Malory re-read with relish—
a gold-green set from Gollancz in the '90s.
(The eighteen-nineties.) But Brocéliande's
now shrunk in Brittany from forest-sorcery.
Intriguing paths that wound towards the Valley
of No Return (risk each time for pure
derision) now tamed by gravel flanked by terse
details of mediaeval fact and legend. These
might baffle any literate knight errant
yet information should be welcome to
the still enquiring mind, for instance by
that Indian Mound in Georgia where you learn
obsidian to chip those arrowheads got lugged
from the Great Lakes and intricate yellow shells
to string a necklace picked up from beaches on
the Gulf hundreds of miles away. Trade-routes
criss-crossing. At Wadi Rum we edged
along the trickle of a stream in one squeezed
canyon the colour of rhubarb. On the walls
merchants over millennia scratched marks.
East-west north-south itineraries
met and parted precisely here. Later
a full moon rose above a cliff and the sand
shone.
            Flying low in that ramshackle plane
over a far greyer desert. Nazca.
No wind or rain so the lines stay clear. Such
generosity. No designer could ever see
the end-result. Spent all that energy
to please the gods who must have smiled fondly
at two-dimensional homage to their own
creative skills for they already knew quite
well what a monkey or a spider looked like.

A week before, up in the Andes, it seemed
Leconte de Lisle was wrong. The first
French poet I really went for. Despairing.
Exotic. Cool master of his craft. What more
could any aspiring poet in his teens
desire? But he—dubbed cruelly by Verlaine
(whom he'd been kind to) in a shortened form
"Le Con"—flew his condor high above the world
to sleep, wings spread, while night rolled like a tide
up snowbound slopes to break in a great wave
of insubstantial ink over its head.
It hung defiant. Never conquered. All
alone. Magnificent. A hero for
the unfledged reader to gasp at. But,
peering into that chasm I was informed
condors roost down close to the swift river
tucked away in caves. I saw one rise, up,
up, into the parched air of morning and set him
beneath the stars unvanquished in my mind,
refusing to let mere proof elbow its way
into the realm where symbols count. A poet's
way with truth.
                    Morgenstern thought his monument
should be a monolith of sugar in the sea.
At low tide's more appropriate. Ray
Bradbury's tale: Picasso's drawing on wet sand—
done for his own delight yet certain
to be effaced by wave succeeding wave.
Goldsworthy plastered a boulder with autumn
leaves to create a red tusk in the water
knowing the stream risen with rainfall
would wash them all away. He naturally took
some photos so the temporary would gain
a permanence transposed. A poem of mine
appeared on the Internet. Where is it

now? Electronically dissipated.
I believe in the book, the written word,
the printed page—in the *library,* even though
successive governments close them down. And now
you often weave a path past stacks of videos—
long-over soccer matches or a new
way to keep fit—before you see the backs
of any books on shelves.
                              The Duchess of Malfi
knew death had ten thousand several doors.
I've seen an image of pure hopelessness.
An atheist's forecast. Tom Courtenay, in a teleplay
adapted from some story by Noël Coward,
died. In bed. One snap of thumb and middle
finger and the screen went blank. He'd gone
and there was nothing. No-one there. From life—
breath, colour, touch—inexorably no
thing left. No void. No state one could define
as emptiness. Not anything you might describe
at all. Merely the loss of everything
that is. For ever. Donne's *Nocturnall* on
the longest nighttime of the year evokes
"absence, darkness, death; things which are not".
A bogeyman for old philosophers
to chill their fingers at. I still find faith
more credible and heartening since a Creator
can uncreate and re-create at will,
bring from pure emptiness a galaxy,
Leviathan, another self. That's anyway
a hopefulness to combat terror in
the small hours, think destruction's not
irreparable—that NEVER as a word
cannot exist.
                    When mortal travelling
at last is over is there the universe

to wander through? To gauge the gravity
on Mars, scale scarlet peaks far loftier
than Everest. See, hanging on to Pluto,
the sun a tiny spark on black and comet-hop
to outer space. I am so limited
I can't conceive of selves who do not need
to read but then who knows in Paradise
how many other ways there are to spend
eternity which must, you'd think, obey
other rules than hours. Forgive the pun.

Jewish thought discourages all idle
speculation on the after-life. It's not
our business. Yet a while. At least.
A guilty pastime though. Which Dante tried.
He took a shot at the ineffable.
And may have missed. Like Milton. Or St. John.

Exeter
April 25th, 2006

CONVERSIONS

Contents

Le Testament XXIX

Ou sont les gracieux gallans
Que je suivoye ou temps jadis,
Si bien chantans, si bien parlans,
Si plaisans en faiz et en dis?
Les aucuns sont morts et roidis,
D'eulx n'est il plus riens maintenant:
Repos aient en paradis,
Et Dieu saulve le remenant!

(François Villon)

LAMENT

Where are those gallants full of grace
Whom I went with in years now gone
So sweet of tongue, so fair of face,
Pleasing in all that's said or done?
Each one in his grave stiffened lies.
They've nothing left on earth at all:
May they find rest in Paradise
And God have mercy on my soul.

Les Regrets xxxi

Heureux qui, comme Ulysse, a fait un beau voyage,
　　Ou comme cestuy là qui conquit la toison,
Et puis est retourné, plein d'usage & raison,
　　Vivre entre ses parents le reste de son aage!

Quand revoiray-je, helas, de mon petit village
　　Fumer la cheminee, & en quelle saison
　　Revoiray-je le clos de ma pauvre maison,
　　Qui m'est une province, & beaucoup d'avantage?

Plus me plaist le sejour qu'ont basty mes ayeux,
　　Que des palais romains le front audacieux,
　　Plus que le marbre dur me plaist l'ardoise fine,

Plus mon Loyre gaulois que le Tybre latin,
　　Plus mon petit Lyré que le mont Palatin,
　　Et plus que l'air marin la doulceur angevine.

(Joachim Du Bellay)

EXPATRIATE

Some fortunate men resemble Ulysses
or Jason, the fleece-winner, both of whom
learned much from voyaging but then turned home
to spend among their own kind years of ease.

When shall I see again the white smoke rise
from neighbouring chimneys—see the plot of land
around my home, a place by no means grand
though worth to me more than ten provinces?

I love far more the house my forebears knew
than these proud palaces stuck up in Rome—
more than hard marble those thin slates of mine—

my gentle slopes more than the Palatine—
my Gallic Loir than Tiber's Latin stream—
more than salt air the softness of Anjou.

SONNET

Comme un qui s'est perdu dans la forest profonde
Loing de chemin, d'oree, et d'adresse, et de gens;
Comme un qui en la mer, grosse d'horribles vens,
Se voit presque engloutir des grans vagues de l'onde:

Comme un qui erre aux champs, lorsque la nuict au monde
Ravit toute clarte, j'avais perdu long temps
Voye, route et lumiere, et presque avec le sens
Perdu long temps l'object, où plus mon heur se fonde.

Mais quand on voit (ayant ces maux fini leur tour)
Aux bois, en mer, aux champs, le bout, le port, le jour,
Ce bien present plus grand que mon mal on vient croire:

Moy donc qui ay tout tel en vostre absence este,
J'oublie en revoyant vostre heureuse clarte,
Forest, tormente et nuict, longue, orageuse et noire.

(Estienne Jodelle)

SONNET

Like someone lost deep in a tangled wood
Far from verge, path, home, trace of humankind—
Like one adrift at sea swayed by the wind
Fearful of sinking in the raging flood—

Like someone straying across fields when night
Is at its darkest, I've lost for so long
My way, my lamp, my bearings—all's gone wrong
Since my beloved's been lost from my sight.

But when you see (once perils fade away)
In woods, at sea, on fields, edge, harbour, day,
Such sudden joy can cancel any threat.

I've learnt throughout your absence all I lack.
Glimpsing again your radiance I forget
Wood, ocean, night—so vast, so rough, so black.

WANDRERS NACHTLIED

I

Über allen Gipfeln
Ist Ruh,
In allen Wipfeln
Spürest du
Kaum einen Hauch;
Die Vögelein schweigen im Walde.
Warte nur, balde
Ruhest du auch.

(Johann Wolfgang von Goethe)

HIGH OVER EVERY HILL...

High over every hill
there's peace.
The woods are all so still
you trace
hardly one breath.
The birds have fallen silent too.
Wait now till you
sleep soft as death.

At the Tomb of Chateaubriand

He recommended
a blunt grey
cross stuck here
against the north.

Green sea
hisses beneath on granite
and the unceasing
gales bring mist.

Under the stone slab
a fleshless head
stares into earth.

Ear-sockets
of crumbling bone
catch the pointless
noise of the living.

Nothing excludes
the tide's return
or the black wind
or the seagull's
questioning cry.

Saint-Malo, April 1978

(Harry Guest)

Au Tombeau de Chateaubriand

Il a recommandé
une croix grise à bouts ronds
fichée ici
contre le nord

La mer verte
ronge le granit
et les rafales
amènent sans cesse l'embrun

Sous la dalle de pierre
une tête sans chair
scrute le sol

Les tympans de l'oreille
dont l'os s'effrite
saisissent le bruit fade
que font les vivants

Rien n'exclut
le retour des marées
ni le vent noirci
ni les questions rauques
posées par la mouette

from DES MEERES UND DER LIEBE WELLEN, ACT 1

Hero

(*ein Körbchen mit Blumen im Arme haltend tritt aus dem
Tempel und steigt die Stufen herab*)

Nun, so weit wär's getan. Geschmückt der Tempel,
Mit Myrt und Rosen ist er rings bestreut
Und harret auf das kommende, das Fest.

Und ich bin dieses Festes Gegenstand.
Mir wird vergönnt, die unbemerkten Tage,
Die fernhin rollen ohne Richt und Ziel,
Dem Dienst der hohen Himmlischen zu weihn;
Die einzelnen, die Wiesenblümchen gleich,
Der Fuß des Wanderers zertritt und knickt,
Zum Kranz gewunden um der Göttin Haupt,
Zu weihen und verklären. Sie und mich.

Wie bin ich glücklich, daß nun heut der Tag;
Und daß der Tag so schön, so still, so lieblich!
Kein Wölkchen trübt das blaue Firmament,
Und Phöbus blickt, dem hellen Meer entstiegen,
Schon über jene Zinnen segnend her.
Schaust du mich schon als Eine von den Euren?
Ward es dir kund, daß jene muntre Hero,
Die du wohl spielen sahst an Tempels Stufen,
Daß sie, ergreifend ihrer Ahnen Recht,
Die Priester gaben von Urväterzeit
Dem hehren Heiligtum—daß sie's ergreifend
Das schöne Vorrecht, Priesterin nun selbst;
Und heute, heut; an diesem, diesem Tage.
Auf jenen Stufen wird das Volk sie sehn
Den Himmlischen der Opfer Gaben spendend.
Von jeder Lippe ringt sich Jubel los,

HERO INTRODUCES HERSELF

Hero
*(Comes down the steps from the Temple,
a basket of flowers on her arm)*

All's done so far. The Temple's decorated
With myrtle-leaves, with roses everywhere,
Anticipating what is still to come.

And I'm the focus for this festival.
I'm to devote what used to be blank time
Unfolding without aim, with no direction,
In service of the Goddess Aphrodite.
And with the days which seemed like meadow-flowers
Crushed by the feet of aimless wayfarers
I'll plait a garland for her statue to
Transfigure and to bless. Her and myself.

How good it is to know to-day's the day—
A lovely one, so clear, so beautiful!
No cloud mars the perfection of blue sky
And Phoebus, rising from the brilliant sea,
Already peers over the Temple roof.
Do you regard me now as one of yours?
Have you been told how that small child you used
To see here playing on the Temple steps
Has claimed the right of all her ancestors?
We've furnished priests almost since time began
To serve this holy place. Now that same child
Has claimed the ancient privilege for herself.
To-day, to-day, this very morning, there
On those white steps, the crowd will watch her while
She offers gifts they've brought to the Immortals.
Then all the people here will shout with joy,

Und in dem Glanz, der Göttin dargebracht,
Strahlt auf der Priestrin Haupt—
                              Allein, wie nur?
Beginn' ich mit Versäumen meinen Dienst?
Hier sind noch Kränze, Blumen hab' ich noch,
Und jene Bilder stehen ungeschmückt?

Hier, Hymenäus, der die Menschen bindet,
Nimm diesen Kranz von Einer, die gern frei.
Die Seelen tauschest du? Ei, gute Götter,
Ich will die meine nur für mich behalten,
Wer weiß, ob eine andre mir so nütz?

Dir Amor sei der zweite meiner Kränze.
Bist du der Göttin Sohn, und ich ihr Kind,
Sind wir verwandt; und redliche Geschwister
Beschädigen sich nicht und halten Ruh.
So sei's mit uns, und ehren will ich dich,
Wie man verehrt, was man auch nicht erkennt.

(Franz Grillparzer)

And, paying homage to the Goddess, see
Light fall on me, the Priestess—
                                    Just a minute!
Am I to start my service with neglect?
Here am I standing, holding all these flowers,
And both those statues wait undecorated.

Hymen unites men with their wives. Accept
This wreath from one who'd sooner stay unwed.
You barter souls, I hear, but, by the Gods,
I far prefer to keep mine for myself.
Would any other be of use to me?

This second garland's for the God of Love.
You're Aphrodite's son and I'm her daughter
So we're related and wise children should
Keep on good terms and never disagree.
The same with us then. I'll respect your ways
And honour what I'll never understand.

Hero *(kommt zurück mit einer Rolle)*
Hier ist dein Brief. Nimmst du ihn nicht?—Ei ja!—
Wo ging er mir nur hin?—Er kommt wohl wieder.
(Sie steckt den Brief in den Gürtel.)
Wie schön du brennst, O Lampe, meine Freundin!
Noch ist's nicht Nacht, und doch geht alles Licht,
Das rings umher die laute Welt erleuchtet,
Von dir aus, dir, du Sonne meiner Nacht.
Wie an der Mutter Brust hängt alles Wesen
An deinem Umkreis, saugend deinen Strahl.

Hier will ich sitzen, will dein Licht bewahren,
Daß es der Wind nicht neidisch mir verlöscht.
Hier ist es kühl, im Turme schwül und schläfrig,
Die dumpfe Luft drückt dort die Augen zu.
Das aber soll nicht sein, es gilt zu wachen.
(Sie sitzt.)
Sie haben mich geplagt den langen Tag
Mit Kommen und mit Gehn. Nicht absichtslos!
Allein weshalb? warum? Ich weiß es nicht.
(Den Kopf in die Hand gesenkt)
Doch immerhin! Drückt erst nicht mehr die Stirn,
Erkenn' ich's wohl. Und dann—soll auch—wenn nur—
(Emporfahrend)
Was ist? Wer kommt?—Ich bin allein. Der Wind nur
Weht schärfer von der See.—So besser denn,
Treibst du den Holden früher ans Gestade.
Die Lampe brennt noch hell. Pfui, wer wird träumen?
Hellauf und frisch! Der Liebe süße Wacht.
(Den Kopf wieder in die Hand gestützt.)
Genau besehn, wollt' ich, er käme nicht.
Ihr Argwohn ist geweckt, sie lauern, spähn.

Hero falls asleep

Hero

I've brought your letter. Don't you want it? Oh!
Now where's my uncle gone?—Well, he'll come back.
> *(She sticks the scroll in her belt.)*
The lamp's my only ally as it shines.
Night hasn't fallen yet. What light there is
To pick out all the objects clothed in dusk
Comes from that lamp, the centre for my darkness.
All nature draws that radiance to itself
Clinging as to a mother's breast for comfort.

I'll sit down here and keep watch to make sure
No grudging breeze extinguishes your light.
It's cool here. In the tower it felt so airless.
My eyes kept closing. I could hardly stay
Awake. But that won't do. I mustn't fall
Asleep.
> *(She sits down.)*
They pestered me all day and sent
Me here and there. Not unintentionally!
But why though? Why? I just don't understand.
> *(She sinks her head on to her hand.)*
And anyway ... If ... When my head stops aching
I'll see why. Then—I should—but only—if—
> *(She starts up.)*
What's that? Who is it? No-one here. The wind's
Blowing more keenly from the sea. That's good!
The waves will drive him faster to this shore.
The lamp's still bright. I haven't time for dreams.
Shine on and keep love company on guard.
> *(Her head once more sinks onto her hand.)*
Strictly I ought to wish him not to come.
They're all suspicious—sneaking round and spying.

Wenn sie ihn träfen—Mitleidsvolle Götter!
Drum wär' es besser wohl, er käme nicht.
Allein er wünscht's, er flehte, bat. Er will's.
Komm immer denn, du guter Jüngling, komm!
Ich will dich hüten, wie der Jungen Schar
Die Glucke schützt, und Niemand soll dir nahn,
Niemand, als ich allein; und nicht zu schäd'gen;
Bewahr! bewahr!—Ich bin doch müd.
Es schmerzt der Fuß. Löst Niemand mir die Schuh?
        (Sie zieht einen Fuß auf die Ruhebank.)
Hier drückt es, hier. Hat mich ein Stein verletzt?
        (Auch den zweiten Fuß an sich ziehend, in halbliegender
        Stellung)
Wie süß, wie wohl!—Komm Wind der Nacht
Und kühle mir das Aug, die heißen Wangen!
Kommst du doch übers Meer, von ihm.
Und, o, dein Rauschen und der Blätter Lispeln,
Wie Worte klingt es mir: von ihm wir, ihm, von ihm.
Breit aus die Schwingen, hülle sie um mich,
Um Stirn und Haupt, den Hals, die müden Arme,
Umfaß, umfang! Ich öffne dir die Brust.—
Und kommt er, sag es an!—Leander—du?

        (Pause)
        (Der Tempelhüter kommt lauschend auf den Zehen.
        Dann tritt der Priester auf.)

Tempelhüter
(sich der Ruhebank nähernd, mit gedämpfter Stimme)

Hero!—Sie schläft.—

Suppose they catch him—May the Gods show mercy!
It would be better if he didn't come.
He wanted to, though—pleaded—begged. He wants to.
Come then. He's so good-looking! Come to me.
I will protect you as a hen cares for
Her flock of chicks and no-one will come near you—
No-one but me. Just me. And not to scold
Or say: "Take care! Take care!" Oh! I'm so tired.
My foot hurts. Ooh! Won't someone take my shoe off?
       (She puts her foot up on to the bench.)
That's where it hurts. Did I pick up a stone?
       (She draws up the other foot and is now half lying.)

That's better. Far more comfortable. When will
The night-wind come to cool my burning face—
Come far across the sea to me from him.
The hiss of waves, the rustling of those leaves—
They sound like whispered words from him—"we come
From him". Spread out your wings, enfold me in them.
Embrace me. Soothe my forehead, soothe my neck,
My tired arms. I offer you my breast.
And when he comes just say—Leander—you?

     (Pause)
     (Enter the Temple Guard on tiptoe, listening.
     He approaches the bench.
     The Priest is visible, standing by the entrance to the tower.)

     Temple Guard *(in a low voice)*
Hero?
     (Turning back towards the Priest)
     Asleep!

Priester

Vom Turme strahlt das Licht.
Der Götter Sturm verlösche deine Flamme!
(Er geht in den Turm.)

Tempelhüter

Was sinnt er nur? Mir wird so bang und schwer.
Wenn ich nicht sprach; und doch, wie konnt' ich anders?
Dort gehen Männer mit des Fischzugs Netzen.
(Sich der rechten Seite nähernd)
Was schafft ihr dort? Ward euch denn nicht geboten,
Zu bleiben heute Nacht dem Meere fern
In eurer Hütten festverschloßnen Räumen?
(Zurückkommend)
Sie meinen, es gibt Sturm. Nun, Götter, waltet!
(Zum Turm emporblickend)
Die Lampe wird bewegt. Er selbst!— Unselig Mädchen!
Erwacht sie? Nein. So warnet dich kein Traum?

Die Lampe verlöscht.

(Hero macht eine Bewegung und sinkt dann tiefer in Schlaf. Das Haupt gleitet aus der unterstützenden Hand und ruht auf dem Oberarm, indes der untere Teil schlaff hinabhängt. Es ist dunkel geworden.)

Mich schaudert. Weh! Hätt' ich mein Oberkleid!

Priester *(kommt zurück.)*
Wer spricht? Bist du's?—Komm mit, es sinkt die Nacht,
Und brütet über ungeschehnen Dingen.
(zu Hero hintretend)
Nun, Himmlische, nun waltet eures Amts!
Die Schuldigen hält Meer und Schlaf gebunden,

Priest
> The lamp shines from the tower.
May the Gods send a storm to put it out.
> *(He enters the tower.)*

Temple Guard
Now what's he up to? I'm afraid. Was I
Too harsh? If I'd not spoken . . . What else could
I do?
> There go men with their fishing nets.
> *(Moves to the right side of the stage)*
What are you doing there? You were all told
Not to come near the shore to-night but stay
Inside your huts with the doors closed.
> *(Coming back)*
> They think
There'll be a storm. Now let the Gods take charge.
> *(He glances up at the tower.)*
The lamp's been moved. It must be him. Poor child.
Is she awake? No. Then no dream has warned you.
> *The lamp goes out.*
(Hero sighs, makes a movement then sinks more deeply in her sleep.
Her head slips from her supporting hand and comes to rest on her arm.
Her hand hangs loose. The stage has grown dark.)

I'm shivering. I wish I'd brought my cloak.

Priest *(re-entering)*
Is that you talking? Let's be off. It's dark.
Night waits to hatch what hasn't happened yet.
> *(Going over to Hero)*
Now let the Gods perform what must be done.
The guilty ones are caught—one by her sleep,

Und so ist eures Priesters Werk vollbracht:
Das Holz geschichtet und das Beil gezückt,
Wend' ich mich ab. Trefft Götter selbst das Opfer!

Indem er sich zum Fortgehen wendet
fällt der Vorhang.

(Franz Grillparzer)

One by the sea. The Priest's work is complete.
The logs are piled. The axe is sharp. I'll leave now.
The Gods alone must sacrifice the victims.

(As he turns to go the curtain falls.)

ICH MÖCHTE, WENN ICH STERBE ...

Ich möchte, wenn ich sterbe, wie die lichten
Gestirne schnell und unbewußt erbleichen,
Erliegen möcht' ich einst des Todes Streichen
Wie Sagen uns von Pindaros berichten.

Ich will ja nicht im Leben oder Dichten
Den großen Unerreichlichen erreichen,
Ich möcht', o Freund, ihm nur im Tode gleichen;
Doch höre nun die schönste der Geschichten.

Er saß im Schauspiel, vom Gesang beweget,
Und hatte, der ermüdet war, die Wangen
Auf seines Lieblings schönes Knie geleget:

Als nun der Chöre Melodien verklangen,
Will wecken ihn, der ihn so sanft geheget,
Doch zu den Göttern war er heimgegangen.

(August Graf von Platen)

The Death of Pindar

Oh, let me, dying, lose my latest breath
As stars turn pale—swift, soft, without a name;
Let my succumbing to the stroke of death
Resemble tales we're told of Pindar's fame.

I would not want in life or art to spend
Time gaining what cannot be gained, although
I'd like to mirror him in death—dear friend,
Hear now the sweetest myth you'll ever know:

He watched the play, moved by each fine refrain,
Till, feeling tired, he laid his cheek upon
The lovely lap of his companion

Who tried, hearing the choric singing cease,
To rouse the man who'd cherished him— in vain—
For he'd gone homeward to the gods in peace.

SPLEEN

Quand le ciel bas et lourd pèse comme un couvercle
Sur l'esprit gémissant en proie aux longs ennuis,
Et que de l'horizon embrassant tout le cercle
Il nous verse un jour noir plus triste que les nuits;

Quand la terre est changée en un cachot humide,
Où l'Espérance, comme une chauve-souris,
S'en va battant les murs de son aile timide
Et se cognant la tête à des plafonds pourris;

Quand la pluie étalant ses immenses traînées
D'une vaste prison imite les barreaux,
Et qu'un peuple muet d'infâmes araignées
Vient tendre ses filets au fond de nos cerveaux,

Des cloches tout à coup sautent avec furie
Et lancent vers le ciel un affreux hurlement,
Ainsi que des esprits errants et sans patrie
Qui se mettent à geindre opiniâtrément.

—Et de longs corbillards, sans tambours ni musique,
Défilent lentement dans mon âme; l'Espoir,
Vaincu, pleure, et l'Angoisse atroce, despotique,
Sur mon crâne incliné plante son drapeau noir.

(Charles Baudelaire)

SPLEEN

When the low sky weighs heavy like a lid
on whimpering souls in their long apathy
and, dark to each horizon, pours a dead
daytime sadder than even night can be;

when earth is altered to a dripping cell
where hope to each trapped captive merely seems
a bat that scrapes one wing against the wall,
flies up and hits its head on rotten beams;

when, imitating prison-bars, the rain
traces interminable lines; and when,
working in silence, hordes of spiders spin
a mesh of evil threads across our brain—

then bells swinging in sudden frenzy hurl
protesting cries to heaven and complain
as wanderers who stray in exile whine
away their endless obstinate appeal.

Long funerals wind slowly though my soul.
No music sounds. No drumroll. All my hopes,
defeated, weep. That despot Anguish drapes
his black flag over my now abject skull.

Le Cygne

à Victor Hugo

I

Andromaque, je pense à vous! Ce petit fleuve,
Pauvre et triste miroir où jadis resplendit
L'immense majesté de vos douleurs de veuve,
Ce Simoïs menteur qui par vos pleurs grandit,

A fécondé soudain ma mémoire fertile,
Comme je traversais le nouveau Carrousel.
Le vieux Paris n'est plus (la forme d'une ville
Change plus vite, hélas! que le coeur d'un mortel);

Je ne vois qu'en esprit tout ce camp de baraques,
Ces tas de chapiteaux ébauchés et de fûts,
Les herbes, les gros blocs verdis par l'eau des flaques,
Et, brillant aux carreaux, le bric-à-brac confus.

Là s'étalait jadis une ménagerie;
Là je vis, un matin, à l'heure où sous les cieux
Froids et clairs le Travail s'éveille, où la voirie
Pousse un sombre ouragan dans l'air silencieux,

Un cygne qui s'était évadé de sa cage,
Et, de ses pieds palmés frottant le pavé sec,
Sur le sol raboteux traînait son blanc plumage.
Près d'un ruisseau sans eau la bête ouvrant le bec

Baignait nerveusement ses ailes dans la poudre,
Et disait, le coeur plein de son beau lac natal:
«Eau, quand donc pleuvras-tu? quand tonneras-tu, foudre?»
Je vois ce malheureux, mythe étrange et fatal,

THE SWAN

to Victor Hugo

I

      I call to mind one stream, Andromache—
      a puny mirror for your sorrow, years
      spent mourning in your widowed majesty.
That mimic Trojan river swollen by your tears

      jogged all at once my fallow memory
      when I crossed the new court close by the Seine.
      Old Paris is no more. A city's sky-
line shifts alas more swiftly than the heart of man.

      Of all that maze of hovels there's no sign.
      I miss those columns rough-hewn in a stack,
      the grass, those blocks in puddles smeared with green,
those criss-crossed window-panes glinting with bric-à-brac.

      And over there sprawled a menagerie.
      Dawn years ago spread cold and clear as men
      were setting off to work. Smoke, acrid, grey,
rose wavering from a rubbish-dump. I saw a swan

      who'd slipped free from its cage go scraping round
      those arid paths on webbed feet dragging white
      plumage along the hard uneven ground.
It reached at last a bone-dry gutter where it sat

      and bathed its wings in dust while gazing up,
      beak gaping, just as though, remembering
      its native lake, it prayed against all hope
for clouds to shroud the sky and rain come thundering.

Vers le ciel quelquefois, comme l'homme d'Ovide,
Vers le ciel ironique et cruellement bleu,
Sur son cou convulsif tendant sa tête avide,
Comme s'il adressait des reproches à Dieu!

II

Paris change, mais rien dans ma mélancolie
N'a bougé! palais neufs, échafaudages, blocs,
Vieux faubourgs, tout pour moi devient allégorie,
Et mes chers souvenirs sont plus lourds que des rocs.

Aussi devant ce Louvre une image m'opprime:
Je pense à mon grand cygne, avec ses gestes fous,
Comme les exilés, ridicule et sublime,
Et rongé d'un désir sans trêve! et puis à vous,

Andromaque, des bras d'un grand époux tombée,
Vil bétail, sous la main du superbe Pyrrhus,
Auprès d'un tombeau vide en extase courbée;
Veuve d'Hector, hélas! et femme d'Hélénus!

Je pense à la négresse, amaigrie et phtisique,
Piétinant dans la boue, et cherchant, l'oeil hagard,
Les cocotiers absents de la superbe Afrique
Derrière la muraille immense du brouillard;

A quiconque a perdu ce qui ne se retrouve
Jamais, jamais! à ceux qui s'abreuvent de pleurs
Et tettent la Douleur comme une bonne louve!
Aux maigres orphelins séchant comme des fleurs!

I see that anguished creature as a new
Promethean emblem twisting up its head
to where the zenith flaunted cruel blue—
a hapless alien offering reproach to God.

II

Paris may change. Nothing in my despair
has stirred. Brash palaces, districts I'd known,
scaffolding—I glimpse symbols everywhere.
Each fond remembrance weighs more heavily than stone.

One image among many occupies
my mind— the frantic action of that swan,
futile, sublime, like any exile who's
corroded ceaselessly by one desire—and then

Andromache, immune once and in love,
who, a mere chattel among spoils of war,
became, though grieving by an empty grave,
a hero's widow doomed to be a wife once more.

That negress too—consumptive, skeletal—
who, stumbling in the mud, strained reddened eyes
to see, past fog forbidding as a wall,
African sunlight on a line of far palm-trees.

Whoever's lost whatever can't again
be salvaged, those who slake their thirst with tears
and suck grief like the teat of some benign
she-wolf or scrawny orphans parching like cut flowers.

Ainsi dans la forêt où mon esprit s'exile
Un vieux Souvenir sonne à plein souffle du cor!
Je pense aux matelots oubliés dans une île,
Aux captifs, aux vaincus! . . . à bien d'autres encor!

(Charles Baudelaire)

The forest where I wander in exile
echoes as ancient memories sound their horn.
I see forgotten sailors on an isle,
captives, the vanquished . . . ah, so many more to mourn.

LE RÊVE D'UN CURIEUX

Connais-tu, comme moi, la douleur savoureuse,
Et de toi fais-tu dire: «Oh! l'homme singulier!»
—J'allais mourir. C'était dans mon âme amoureuse,
Désir mêlé d'horreur, un mal particulier;

Angoisse et vif espoir, sans humeur factieuse.
Plus allait se vidant le fatal sablier,
Plus ma torture était âpre et délicieuse;
Tout mon coeur s'arrachait au monde familier.

J'étais comme l'enfant avide du spectacle,
Haïssant le rideau comme on hait un obstacle . . .
Enfin la vérité froide se révéla:

J'étais mort sans surprise, et la terrible aurore
M'enveloppait.—Eh quoi! n'est-ce donc que cela?
La toile était levée et j'attendais encore.

(Charles Baudelaire)

THE DREAM OF A CURIOUS MAN

Do you, like me, find pain tastes sweet and sour?
Do people say of you "He's an odd cove!"
I lay near death. My soul, though stocked with love,
ran a strange malady: desire plus fear—

anguish—barbed hope—no urge for contumely.
Sand, trickling swiftly through Fate's hour-glass, drew
harsher enticement to my agony.
My heart had been prised loose from all I knew.

Like some child at the play I sat there hating
that wretched curtain as a hindrance . . . but
the chilling truth became clear all too soon.

I'd died without surprise and the dread dawn
enfolded me. "What! Do you mean that's *it?*"
The curtain had gone up. I was still waiting.

MONTE SUR MOI COMME UNE FEMME . . .

Monte sur moi comme une femme
Que je baiserais en gamin.
Là. C'est cela. T'es à ta main?
Tandis que mon vit t'entre, lame

Dans du beurre, du moins ainsi
Je puis te baiser sur la bouche,
Te faire une langue farouche
Et cochonne, et si douce, aussi!

Je vois tes yeux auxquels je plonge
Les miens, jusqu'au fond de ton coeur,
D'où mon désir revient vainqueur
Dans une luxure de songe.

Je caresse le dos nerveux,
Les flancs ardents et frais, la nuque,
La double mignonne perruque
Des aisselles et les cheveux!

Ton cul à cheval sur mes cuisses
Les pénètre de son doux poids
Pendant que s'ébat mon lourdois
Aux fins que tu te réjouisses.

Et tu te réjouis, petit,
Car voici que ta belle gaule,
Jalouse aussi d'avoir son rôle,
Vite, vite, gonfle, grandit,

Raidit . . . Ciel! la goutte, la perle
Avant-courrière, vient briller

CLIMB ON ME AS A WOMAN MIGHT . . .

Climb on me as a woman might
whom I'd then lift my lips to kiss.
Yes, that's it! Wouldn't do to miss!
My cock will enter you just right

(a blade up butter) and this way
I get to kiss you on the mouth—
your wild exploring tongue moves south,
mine north, they meet, how sweet, how gay.

I see your eyes. My longing gaze
reaches the heart of you where my
inventive lechery will try
to take you seventy different ways.

My hands caress your supple back,
stroke all of you, ardent, your nape,
cool sides and those moist tufts that shape
your armpits—like your hair, silk-black.

Your buttocks now astride my thighs,
I sense their soft weight while my tool
thrusts up you making certain you'll
find my enjoyment gratifies

us both. Look! Your enjoyment shows!
Wanting its turn your splendid prick
flaunts its own eagerness—so thick,
so stiff—and thicker still it grows—

still stiffer . . . There! A pearl! It gets
a hint of what's to come, a drop

Au méat rose: l'avaler,
Moi, je le dois, puisque déferle

Le mien de flux. Or c'est mon lot
De faire tôt d'avoir aux lèvres
Ton gland chéri tout lourd de fièvres
Qu'il décharge en un royal flot.

Lait suprême, divin phosphore
Sentant bon la fleur d'amandier,
Où vient l'âpre soif mendier
La soif de toi qui me dévore.

Mais il va, riche et généreux,
Le don de ton adolescence,
Communiant, de ton essence,
Tout mon être ivre d'être heureux.

(Paul Verlaine, from *Hombres*)

glinting at its pink lip—No! Stop!
I want to taste it . . . Aaahh! Mine jets

right up you, flooding. Now I speed
to have that succulent knob of yours
between my lips. Spurting it pours
rich sperm to satisfy my greed—

milk, perfect, creamlike, heavenly,
smelling of almond-blossom, so
harsh thirst must beg with head held low.
My thirst for you obsesses me.

Still, well-endowed and generous,
you never fail, sweet youth, to slake
me with those gifts you have and make
me drunk again with happiness.

DER LATTENZAUN

Es war einmal ein Lattenzaun,
mit Zwischenraum, hindurchzuschaun.

Ein Architekt, der dieses sah,
stand eines Abends plötzlich da—

und nahm den Zwischenraum heraus
und baute draus ein großes Haus.

Der Zaun indessen stand ganz dumm,
mit Latten ohne was herum.

Ein Anblick gräßlich und gemein.
Drum zog ihn der Senat auch ein.

Der Architekt jedoch entfloh
nach Afri – od – Ameriko.

(Christian Morgenstern)

The Lattice-Fence

A lattice-fence that I once knew
had spaces you could see right through.

An architect passed by one night
and, fascinated by the sight,

took all the spaces one by one
and built a house second to none.

The fence bewildered stood its ground
with lattices but nothing round—

a nasty sight (and vulgar) so
the Council said it had to go.

The architect though fled away
to Afric– or Americay.

HERBSTTAG

Herr; es ist Zeit. Der Sommer war sehr groß.
Leg deinen Schatten auf die Sonnenuhren,
und auf den Fluren laß die Winde los.

Befiehl den letzten Früchten voll zu sein;
gib ihnen noch zwei südlichere Tage,
dränge sie zur Vollendung hin und jage
die letzte Süße in den schweren Wein.

Wer jetzt kein Haus hat, baut sich keinen mehr.
Wer jetzt allein ist, wird es lange bleiben,
wird wachen, lesen, lange Briefe schreiben
und wird in den Alleen hin und her
unruhig wandern, wenn die Blätter treiben.

(Rainer Maria Rilke)

Autumn Day

It's time now, Lord. The summer was immense.
Replace your shadow on the sundials, let
The winds flow over fields in recompense.

The southward sun needs two more days to shine.
Tell the last fruits what they have to fulfil.
Urge them towards completion till they spill
All the last sweetness into heavy wine.

Who has no house won't start to build one now.
Who's still alone will have to stay that way,
Will wake and read and write long letters, stray
Along the avenues and wonder how
Uneasily the dry leaves ricochet.

Two "E"less Conversions

for Timothy Adès, Master of the lipogram

1. Shak★sp★ar★: Sonn★t XVIII

Shall I say thy looks match a sun-struck day?
Thou art too tranquil and too glorious.
Rough winds lash out at darling buds in May;
Warm months pass all too rapidly for us.

That orb which gilds our sky at noon can burn—
Apollo's brows may frown till day falls dim—
What's fair, alas, from fair at last must turn
As luck will shift or fatal scissors trim.

But thy immortal glamour cannot fail
Nor will thy quality succumb to harm—
No tomb can brag that thou art in its gaol
For my undying stanzas guard thy charm.

So long as man owns lungs and has his sight
So long wilt thou within this song stay bright.

2. K★ats: Od★ to a Nightingal★ v.1

My mind hurts and a drowsy poison pains
    My soul as though of opium I had drunk
Or, quaffing a dull drug down to its drains
    An hour ago, to Pluto's lands had sunk.
'Tis not through craving for thy happy lot
    But finding too much joy in all thy bliss—
        O thou, light-flying dryad of this wood,
          In a harmonious plot
    Of mossy boughs which shift as shadows kiss
        Thy full throat sings May harbours all that's good.

www.ingramcontent.com/pod-product-compliance
Lightning Source LLC
Chambersburg PA
CBHW022206080426
42734CB00006B/572